How To Create Your Own TV Talk Show

By: Tyrik Wynn

COPYRIGHT ©2020

Acknowledgments

I want to thank the following radio and TV personalities for their support and encouragement Shon Gables, Shana Thornton, Denise Dillon, Rashad Richey, Sharon Reed, Jovita Moore, Francesca Amiker, Vince Sims, Mike Dunston, Fred Blankenship, Fago Franklin, Judge Lauren Lake, Alicia Roberts, Nicole Carr, Hope Ford, Nick Sturdivant, Kerry Charles, Ryan Bessley, Mann Robinson, Natasha Lee, Brittany Miller, Frank Ski, Maria Boynton, Amanda Cooper, Tracye Hutchins, Tamron Hall and her producers and many more.

I want to thank my former schoolteachers for teaching me the skills that I needed to be on this journey, for believing in me and for supporting me.

To all of the guests who have come on *Tyrik On The Move*, thanks for being a part of the show and helping it grow.

Thank you to all of the fans of the show, your likes, comments and views are very meaningful to me.

A big thank you to my family and friends, I could not have done it without you all.

Thank you, Marcus Williams at Nubian Bookstore, for allowing me to have my first book in your bookstore and allowing me to host many book signings and meet & greets.

Special thanks you to all of the *Tyrik On The Move* advertisers and sponsors, you keep the show going.

Huge thanks to all of my Panther Report News colleagues at Georgia State University and my NABJ-GSU family.

Thank you 21st Century Leaders for accepting me to the camp of a lifetime, Turner Voices Youth Media Institute. It was one of the greatest experiences of my life and it helped me enhance my television skills.

I want to give a big shout out to Michelle Amara, the President of SCB Video TV Marketing, for not only giving me my first internship, but for also making my television dreams come to a reality.

I also want to give a big huge shout out to my parents, Tilik & Katrina Wynn for helping me through all of this, for leading me down the road to success, and for being the best parents a child could have. Finally, I want to give the biggest shout out and thank you to God, who is the head of my life. I have been so blessed throughout my entire life.

Table of Contents

Introduction

Chapter 1: Who is Your Audience?

Chapter: 2: What Will You Talk About?

Chapter 3: How to Make a TV Show Treatment & What Legal Stuff You Need

Chapter 4: What Equipment and People Do You Need?

Chapter 5: Make Your Content Viewable

Chapter 6: How to Make Money

Chapter 7: How to Apply for Media Credentials

Chapter 8: How to Get Celebrity Interviews

About the Author

Introduction

Hello everyone! It's the youngest TV talk show host, Tyrik Wynn. I am very happy and grateful, that you are investing in your future by reading this phenomenal book. I have been asked numerous times, how I created my TV talk show and how I get to interview these big-time celebrities. Well, I finally decided to put some of my knowledge into a book, so other people can have this valuable information and use their talents to get creative.

The name of my show is called *Tyrik On The Move*. I started my show back in 2016 at 16 years old. At 14 years old I wrote my first book along with my mom entitled *Green Is The Thing! Money Management For Kids*. That book gained lots of traction, and I was invited to do interviews on radio shows and LIVE TV about the book. By being invited to do interviews, is how I gained the passion to have my own platform and to be on television. I told my parents that I had an idea for my show, and I wanted to take it straight to television. They told me that it was not that easy because if it was, then plenty of people would have their show on TV. My parents said that I should start by creating my own YouTube Channel because many people have been discovered through YouTube. So, I went and created my own YouTube channel, and started my show. In the beginning it was not that great. I started with a blurry Nikon camera, a small tripod, a toy microphone that everyone laughed at, and no talk show hosting experience.

    On down the road I started studying my craft, watching other hosts on television, and then once my parents saw I was serious about this, they bought me better equipment and from there, my talent got better, the show got better, viewership started to go up and more. Right now, I will say, I am at a great place with my show and my company, but there is still a lot of work to be done and plenty of goals and milestones I want to achieve.

In this book you will learn how to create your own TV talk show, how to make money with your show, how to get celebrity interviews, how to get into big-time events and more. I hope you enjoy reading this book!

Who Is Your Audience?

Before you can begin to create your own TV talk show, you need to figure out who your audience is. Take time and ask yourself, what demographic do I want to reach and appeal to? The best way to do that, is to categorize it by age or gender. I recommend choosing a group you are associated with or already knowledgeable about, that way you have credibility within your content.

Examples:

The Different Age Groups:

- Kids: 3 to 12 years old
- Teenagers/Young Adults: 13 to 21 years old
- Millennials: 22 to 38 years old
- Older Population: 39 years old and up
- All: 8 to 80

Other Groups You Can Potentially Reach:

- Married Couples
- Single Moms

- Politicians
- Entrepreneurs/Aspiring Entrepreneurs
- 9 to 5 Workers
- People Who Like to Cook
- Victims of Certain Life Issues

Once you figure out the specific audience you want to reach and what you want to discuss on your show, then you can begin to brainstorm what content you will provide for your audience.

What Will You Talk About?

Now that you have figured out who your audience is, it's time to develop content for your show. Go back and look to see who your audience is, based off of that, you can choose your content. If you are having trouble figuring out what to talk about and how to keep viewers entertained, discuss on your show certain life issues that your audience may face.

For example, if your audience consist of children, some children face bullying in school. If you talk about bullying, and how to prevent it, and how to stand up to a bully, kids will be more inclined to tune in and watch your show. If you have a show and you want to cater to entrepreneurs, figure out what entrepreneurs want to hear. Entrepreneurs want to know how they can make more money within their business, ways to pay less taxes during tax time, how to get reliable employees, and more.

If your show is geared towards teenagers, talk about issues that teens face today. Teenagers often face depression, peer pressure from social media, etc.

I recommend, based on your targeted audience, to do research and figure out what things are going on within their realm. You can also take a survey from your target audience. Ask your target audience what they find entertaining, what issues do they face, what shows do they watch on TV, what are some of their hobbies. Once you take a survey, collect the data, and then you will be able to analyze what you will talk about on your show, the segments you will have, and the guests you will bring on.

If you are going to interview someone make sure you research the person before you coordinate the interview. Make the person feel like they are important. If you are talking about any particular subject on your show, make you are knowledgeable about it, or bring someone on the show to educate the audience.

How to Make a TV Show Treatment and What Legal Stuff You Need

The TV show treatment is one of the most important parts of your show. If you don't have a registered TV show treatment someone could steal your idea, and all of the hard work you put into creating your program. Writing a treatment is easy and simple.

When you are writing a show treatment it should be in "courier" 12pt font. Make sure to put the copyright symbol and year at the top of the treatment.

Elements of a TV show treatment (In order):

- Author Name: In this space you put the first and last name of the author of the show. Who is the genius behind the content; the creator?

- Genre: In this space you put the genre of your show you are creating. What kind of show is it; talk show, reality series, etc.
- Logline: Here you put what other shows are similar to your show? Pick 2. (ex. "Shark Tank" meets the "The Profit") Then do a short description of what your show is about.
- Synopsis: A longer description of what your show will be about; what will happen; what will take place? Where the show will be filmed. Go into deep detail, this is where you get to tell people what is going to be in your show.

Once you have created your show treatment, you should register it with the "Writers Guild of America", (they have an east coast office and a west coast office) and also register it with, the "US Copyright Office". You can visit the website for each to see the fees and the process of how to register your work. It is an easy and simple process.

When you create your show, at some point you will run into contracts and disclosures. Have an entertainment attorney on your team. Discuss with them any disclosures that people may ask you to sign. Anytime I am being asked to sign any documents they go to my attorney first. My attorney takes about 1 to 2 business days to look over any paperwork and then they send it back and break down the legal terms that I may not understand.

If you want disclosures for your platform, then you and your attorney need to make some for your show. It's very important to have your own documents. For example, sometimes on my talk show we will film at certain locations. One time I taped an episode of my show, at a well-known, international establishment. We discussed with them that we needed a disclosure signed that states, we had permission to film inside and outside the location, to film their representative, and that we are liable for our equipment, but they would be liable if someone from their establishment damaged anything. They also, put up a sign on the day of filming, to let their customers know that they may be on camera, if they come inside the building. In these disclosures, you should also make sure that you put in information regarding any fees that may or may not be paid to people that are being filmed, who has control over-edited images, and who owns the final product. Which in many cases you will make sure that you have ownership and the final say, since this is your show.

If you are filming outside of your home or studio, make sure to check to see if you need a permit. There are some public places you may need a permit to film at. For example, you may be able to film on a college campus, but areas like the library may require you to apply for a filming permit. Once you apply for the permit and they approve you and give you the days and time they will allow filming, you can start filming at that specific location. If you don't have a filming permit for a location you are filming at, and it is considered private property, you will probably be asked to leave or they will tell you that you need a permit to film at that location. It happened to me a few times when I first started in the industry. There are many places that you make think are public and you are free to film there but, it turns out to be private property. Now that I have educated myself, I have more knowledge about these things, and I am more careful when I film.

When filming people, you should also be very careful. Even though it seems like everyone wants to be a celebrity these days, not everyone wants to be on film. When I am filming my show, if we are at an event where media is present, then people have already been informed either on their ticket or signage throughout the venue that filming is taking place. If I am filming in a public place, we put up signage near where the filming is taking place, so if they do not want to be on camera, then they just have to avoid coming near where I am filming the show. There have been instances where we have been on private property and people have told us that they did not want to be filmed, so we blocked off an area for us to film, and if we happen to get them on film, we try to edit them out. The best thing to do is to get anyone who is going to be on your show, to sign a disclosure that gives you consent to film them.

    Also, look into getting insurance, because some facilities and locations may require you to have it. Contact an insurance company to see what type of insurance you may need and what it will cost you.

What Equipment & People Do You Need?

To have a good quality TV talk show, you will need the right equipment to make the production run smooth. The equipment depends upon your budget and how much you would like to spend.

List of basic equipment needed to run a TV show production:

- Camera (HD or higher quality)
- Lavalier microphones & Hardwire microphone
- Tripod
- Headphones
- Lighting
- Green screen (Optional)
- Editing software: Premiere Pro/Final Cut

All of these items can be ordered online on Amazon, or you can go to film and camera stores in your community to purchase these items. I recommend making the biggest investment in your camera. You want to make sure you invest in a camera that is clear with good quality, easy to operate or easy to learn how to operate, has more than one microphone output, and have one that you can plug in and charge. I shoot all of my shows and productions with a Cannon HD XA11 video camera.

The second biggest investment you need to make, is in your microphones. Videos without good sound quality are not worth showing. When I first started, I made the mistake of not having good quality microphones, I used a toy microphone that I had from a kid's meal from a fast-food restaurant. Remember, I was a teenager without a job and my parents had not started investing in my career yet, because they did not know if I was just doing it for a hobby, or if I was serious about being a journalist. After a few months with bad sound quality and me showing that I was serious about being a journalist, my parents invested in microphones, additional cameras, lighting, and even a green screen.

There are a few types of microphones you can buy. I recommend buying lavalier microphones and handheld hardwire microphones. When you are coordinating scheduled sit-down interviews, you want to have a lavalier microphone on you and the interviewee. Make sure both mics are on and do a sound test before you begin interviewing. If you are doing red carpet interviews or out in the field shooting, then you want to use a handheld hardwire microphone.

While we are talking about microphones and sound, we also need to discuss headphones. A good set of headphones is important, because while the camera person is filming, they can hear what the microphones are picking up and if the sound quality is good. If while your camera person is filming and something happens to the sound, they will notice, and they can try to fix the problem on the spot. If you don't have headphones for the camera person and something happens to the sound, you won't know until you look back at the footage, and depending on what you are filming, you may not be able to look at it until you are ready to edit. I have had many sound issues happen while taping my show and having headphones was a lifesaver because I was able to reshoot while we were on location.

A tripod is also a great investment because when you are filming your show, you want your video steady and not shaky. People tend to tune out and not watch content if there is a shaky video involved. The tripod is also useful if you ever end up filming your show by yourself. You can set up the camera and tripod and step in front of the camera and film yourself. Make sure to get a reliable and sturdy tripod with strong legs. Be sure that the tripod you buy goes up to your own desired height.

Everybody needs good lighting, when you are on air, you want your face to show up clearly. Lighting is your best friend when you go out and shoot at various locations, they won't always have the best light, which is why you need to have lighting that can go on top of your camera. If you are like me, and you have an in-home studio then you want to buy a lighting package. The typical lighting packages come with 4 lighting stands, 4 big bulbs, and 4 bulb covers. There are various lighting packages and lights for your camera, so research to find the one that works best for you.

Depending on what type of show you have and what atmosphere you want, a green screen is optional. I have a green screen because I like to use different backgrounds on my show. Also, if my interviewee is not local, I do a skype interview with them in front of the green screen and it makes the content more exciting when you have a nice background.

Last, but not least, you need to have great editing software. The two best editing software programs in my opinion, are Adobe Premiere Pro and Final Cut. I use Adobe Premiere Pro to edit all of my broadcasts. I think it's very easy and simple. I have not had the pleasure of using Final Cut, but I know plenty of people who have, and they say it is a great editing program also. These editing programs can be costly, but some of them, you can get for a small monthly fee. If you do decide to use Final Cut or Premiere Pro, go online, sign up, pay, and download the apps. Once you download the apps learn how to use it by watching a few YouTube videos until you get the hang of it or you can sign up for editing learning classes.

  If any of these items, from the camera to the editing program is not in your budget when you first start, then you can always film your show on your iPhone and use iMovie to edit. Many of the iPhones within the past few years have great cameras, sound, and lighting. iMovie is a free and easy app that you can use for editing.

  If you are ready to invest in equipment or already have the equipment, then you can start to set up your team of dedicated people to help you with your show.

Team of people needed:

- Host(s)
- Camera Person
- Producer
- Graphic designer
- Writer
- Editor

    I would recommend finding college students that are majoring in filming or other similar fields to assist you with these positions. They have some knowledge and they would love to get the experience. Plus, they would be less expensive to hire, than someone who is doing this as a career already. You should also check to see if people in your family would be interested in helping you out and ask friends if they would like to be on a part of the production. If you do have money in your budget and you want to let someone else film and produce your show, then you can call the professionals, Wynn Productions LLC at (754) 225-

2805. Yes, this is my company, we specialize in producing television shows and other production needs that you may have.

Make Your Content Viewable

Now that you have all the basic essentials to start a TV talk show, it's time to learn how to make your content viewable so people can watch it.

Platforms where you can post your content:
- YouTube
- Facebook
- Instagram
- ROKU TV
- Amazon Fire TV
- LinkedIn
- Vimeo
- Local Cable TV

These are some of the basic platforms where you can broadcast your show. The first platform where you want to start broadcasting your show is YouTube. Many people have been discovered through YouTube and you could be next! If you do not know how to set up a YouTube Channel, do not worry, I will show you how in the steps below.

Step-By-Step process to make a YouTube Channel:

- Go on your internet browser and go to google.com.
- Click the sign-in button in the top corner.
- Click create account.
- Choose "For myself" or "To manage my business."
- Fill in the slots with your information that Google requests, then hit next.
- Verify your phone number, then hit next.
- Google will send a text to your phone with a code. Type that code in and hit next.
- Then enter all the required info on the next page.
- Once that is complete Google will take you back to the home google page, when you get there

click on the icon with the 9 boxes. There will be choices that appear, click the one that says YouTube.

- Once it takes you to YouTube, click the icon in the top right-hand corner and sign into your account.
- Once you sign in click create a YouTube channel, and then your channel will be created, and you can fill it up with videos and episodes of your show.

Once you have your YouTube Channel, go and make professional social media pages with your show title on them. You can also post your show videos on these platforms, like Facebook, LinkedIn, and Instagram. Just know the rules and video limitations for each of these platforms.

Once you have taped a few shows and you plan on continuing to do the show, then you may want to look into taking it to television. There are a few approaches to doing this. You can make your own ROKU channel. All you have to do is go to the ROKU developer website, developer.roku.com, contact ROKU and ask, or you can look it up on YouTube. If you don't want to create your own ROKU channel, see if you can find any ROKU channel owners, that may allow other people to air their content on their ROKU channel. Once you find a channel owner that is willing to do this, then make sure that you have a contract written up that will specify who owns the content, when it will air, who will upload it, and any other specifics. Once your show is on ROKU, continue to upload content to keep it fresh and to keep people interested in viewing it.

You should also look into getting your show on local cable channels in your area. Look for the channels in your area, find out who the station manager, or content manager is for that station, and discuss with them how to get your show on their channel.

If you are interested in getting your show on national television that will require more steps and can involve investing more money. One thing that you need to have ready, is a sizzle reel and a pilot episode. A sizzle reel is a short video that highlights what your show is about. Most sizzle reels are under two minutes, but you should research to see how long it should be for the type of show that you have and what should be highlighted. The pilot episode is the first episode that introduces you to the audience and what the show is about.

Many people have used agents to shop their show to different networks and the networks can decide if they are interested in your show. Hiring an agent is expensive and does not always guarantee that your show will be picked up by a network. Also, if you know people in high places, network, and use your plugs and connections, and let them know about your show because they may be able to get you with the right people to get you on local or national television.

How To Make Money With Your Show

While your show is still on social network platforms, Roku, and local cable channels, you can work on getting advertisers and sponsors. Advertisers and sponsors are people who pay you, to run ads forthem on your show. When you are on national television, it will work differently and the fee for advertising will be much higher.

Before you begin to contact businesses about doing advertising, you have to create packages for the customer to review. When you have packages with pricing and information on them, it makes you look good in front of the potential customer and they are more likely to do business with you. Your packages should include the following: what you are offering, your pricing for your services, how long their ad will air, how customers can pay you, turnaround time for that certain service, and where they can see your content. Also, you need to have a contract or agreement the customer will sign, that way you all are on the same page during the process.

If you have a team of people working with you, like I do, then you can create these commercials for the advertiser, if this is something that you have the skills and ability to do. This is another stream of income on top of them paying for the commercial to air during your show. Most businesses use commercials to get the word out about their business and inform people about what they are selling.

If you don't want to get involved with commercials, you can still make money by doing other forms of advertising on your show. For example, you can make a graphic for a business, and the graphic can have all of their information on it, and then you play music over the graphic, and that can be an ad. Also, if you have a clothing company that decides to advertise with you, you can wear their clothes on your show, and they can be your fashion sponsor. You can also look to charge people for you interviewing them on your show. If someone is a business owner, you can go to their business location, interview them on your show, and they can pay for it to air on one or two broadcasts.

  When going after businesses to advertise, you need to have a master game plan in place to be successful in this area. I have a few strategies I use to get customers. I contact all the entrepreneurs I know and ask them to advertise and support my show. The people that you are close with will sometimes be more inclined to support you, rather than people you don't know. If you get no's from those people, don't be discouraged, there are more strategies and tactics you can take. Next, you can contact small businesses in your county and city. When you contact them let them know you are local, just like they are, and you want to help them boost their business. Local small business owners will be more inclined to do business with you if you are local and you have good viewership on your show. Another strategy is to get local magazines and look through them to see what businesses are advertising in them, pay attention to billboards on the road, look at businesses that advertise on television and contact them. You want to contact these people because they are already advertising, and they could potentially have a big marketing budget. This strategy will most likely give you the most success when you are looking for advertisers and sponsors.

Once you get a few businesses to advertise, make it known on social media that these businesses are advertising with you. Once people on social media see that people are doing business with you, then other businesses are more inclined to advertise with you.

After a business' ad time is up, give them a free incentive. For example, post their ad on your social media page or air their ad for another week for free. When you do extra things for the customer, they will be more likely to renew their agreement with you and will continue to be a returning customer.

How to Apply for Media Credentials

As an established media outlet, you have the ability to go to all kinds of events, and you can cover them and get in free by obtaining media credentials for an event. This is where you can use your media outlet perks. Some of your best content for your show will come from events, if you decide to cover them.

Before you can start covering events, you have to gain established and consistent viewership, and you have to consistently put out content.

Step-by-step process on applying for media credentials:

- A year prior, write down all the events you would like to get media credentials too.
- Log on to Google and type in the event name and then after that, type in media credentials. Usually when you Google media credentials for an event

it will take you to that event's press page and they will have the credential application and information on the event and a contact email and/or phone number. If the credential application doesn't open up until a certain date, then make note of that on your list and set an electronic reminder to apply for media credentials the day of. Being one of the first media outlets to apply for media credentials will up your chances of getting accepted into the event.

- If you come across the media credential application, fill out the application in its entirety. A complete application is a must, to be considered for access to the event. The person over the press credentials sometimes will base their decision on your viewership, your reach, and circulation. The more viewers you have, the better chance you have to get in. If there is a space for viewership and circulation on the application, add up all of your analytics on each platform where people can see your content, count all views, then put that number in.

- Submit the application and make a record that you applied for media credentials for that event.
- If a few weeks have passed and you haven't heard anything back from the event staff for media credentials, do a follow-up email with the person over credentials. By sending this, it will show that you are on top of your business, and you are looking forward to the event. This could also enhance your chances of getting into the event.
- Wait on the acceptance email. If you, unfortunately, get denied media credentials for an event, don't get discouraged, it probably was not meant to be, and God has something better in store for you. Plus, you can always apply for the next year.

How to Get Celebrity Interviews

Interviewing celebrities on your show will drive many people to your content. This happened for me, at first my talk show, *Tyrik On The Move* was a show where I only interviewed business owners, but unfortunately, I did not have a high viewership rate, so I had to change up my show. When I started interviewing celebrities on my show, my viewership grew, my social media presence blossomed, and I became more well known around town. Although, getting celebrities to appear on your show may be difficult, it is not impossible, all you have to do is get in touch with the right people and you just might be successful.

Step-by-step process to get celebrity interviews:

- Make a list of all the celebrities you want to appear on the show.
- Go on the internet and log onto IMDB.com. IMDB is a website that almost all celebrities are on. This website provides contact information for a celebrity's staff.
- Click on the button that says IMDB Pro. Make an account under IMDB Pro. This program will give you a 30-day free trial, and then will charge you a monthly fee of $19.99. You cancel your membership at any time even before it starts to charge you.
- After you make the account, then you will have access to all the information you need to book a celebrity for an interview on your show.
- Go in the IMDB Pro search engine, and type in a celebrity's name from your list and hit enter. Scroll down and look for the celebrity's publicist. The publicist is the person who lets the media

know what their client is working on, and they book all of their media-related gigs.

- Under the publicist section it will have their name, phone number and/or email address. Copy and paste their email address into your composed email. Type up an email, and let the publicist know your outlet name, the celebrity interview you are requesting, information about your media outlet, information about you and other additional information you think they should know.

- Continue to do this for every celebrity you would like to interview. Keep in mind, celebrities have very busy schedules and some of them will say no to interviewing with you, but don't get discouraged every interview that is meant for you to get, you will get it.

This is the key factor to take your show to the top. Also, when various networks see you have connections to celebrity publicists, your journey to a television network may be a little easier.

I want to hear your success stories. Send me an email at tyrikwynntv@gmail.com I receive a very high volume of emails daily, so it may take a little while for me to get to your email, but I'll do my best to reply to as many as I can.

Good luck on creating your own TV talk show. Be blessed and thanks for reading my book. I hope you got some very valuable information out of this book. Once again, if you want your own show, but want to lighten your workload, then contact Wynn Productions LLC, "It's A Wynn Wynn Situation!"

Brainstorm Your Show Ideas

About the Author

Tyrik Wynn is an outstanding 19-year-old author. He wrote his first book at the age of 14 along with his mother, T.Wynn as the co-author, entitled *Green Is The Thing! Money Management For Kids.* Their book is designed to teach the youth about the importance of finances at an early age. Their book is available on amazon.com barnesandnoble.com, Nubian Bookstore, and other various book websites.

Tyrik is the owner and CEO of Wynn Productions LLC. Wynn Productions LLC specializes in video production, TV shows, commercials, general videos, "V-Cards" also known as video business cards and more. All the shows and broadcasts, that are put out by Tyrik, are produced by Wynn Productions LLC.

He is also, an astonishing talk show host. The name of his show is *Tyrik On The Move,* which he started in September of 2016. His show is geared towards anyone who likes fun and positivity. On *Tyrik*

On The Move, Tyrik covers various events and places, such as events happening inside the NFL, family-friendly fun places, festivals and so much more. When he is at these events, Tyrik interacts and interviews many of the participants and leaders associated with the event or place. Not only that, but Tyrik also has conducted many must-watch interviews with various high-profile public figures on his show. He's interviewed 2020 Presidential Candidates Andrew Yang, Tom Steyer, and Cory Booker. Tyrik has also interviewed Congressman John Lewis, Tenzing Norgay Trainor, Jason Earles, Sierra McCormick, Anthony Hamilton, TV Judge Lauren Lake, Christian Rap Artist Lecrae, Super Bowl Champion Tyrone Keys, Saints QB Drew Brees, Hall of Famer Tony Gonzalez, Saints Kicker Wil Lutz, Ravens QB Lamar Jackson, Radio Host Larry Tinsley, Hawks PG Trae Young, News Anchor Sharon Reed, Boxer Gervonta Tank Davis, Steelers Corner Joe Haden, Browns TE Austin Hooper, Seahawks cornerback Shaquill Griffin,

Radio Host Frank Ski, Hall of Famer Ed Reed, Broadcaster Mike Hill, Atlanta Mayor Keisha Lance Bottoms and many more. Also, during the show, he speaks on an array of topics, and he keeps his viewers informed, all while giving terrific tips to his audience whether they are young or old. His show offers something for everyone.

He has also co-hosted an episode of *Real Talk with Rashad Richey* on News and Talk 1380WAOK/V-103 HD3, which is a radio station in Atlanta, GA. During that episode Rashad Richey interviewed Tyrik about some of his accomplishments as a young individual. After the interview, Tyrik was invited to co-host an episode. They discussed politics, music, and current events, and they even took calls from viewers. Another fun fact, Tyrik has been interviewed by Tamron Hall, on the Tamron Hall Show and they added a small clip of his interview in her show introduction, during the time she was taping her show from home, during the pandemic.

Tyrik is a field reporter and intern with a local television station in Henry County, SCB Video TV Marketing. He does field reports for the news station, schedules production shoots, and operates their social media. He is currently the youngest reporter for that station. He has starred in many of their commercials as an actor and as a voice over talent. Not only that, Tyrik is a judge on the kids baking TV show, *Kids Baking Battle,* it can be watched on Antenna Channel 21.1, Roku, Amazon Fire TV, Facebook, Atlanta CW69, and other various places.

Tyrik Wynn is a student at Georgia State University where he is majoring in journalism, to fulfill his career in the television industry. He is an award-winning news anchor, reporter and sports analyst for Georgia State University's news station, *Panther Report News*. At *Panther Report News*, Tyrik has interviewed many people, has covered political rallies, covered the Gubernatorial race, GSU football, the coronavirus pandemic, the Atlanta Hawks and much more. Every year the news team at Georgia State goes to compete in SEJC (Southeast Journalism Conference). Tyrik has won 1st place for "Best Hard News Reporter" in the southeast region and 2nd place for "Current Events." He has accepted a position as the new Executive Producer for the news. Not only that, but he was also recently elected as the President for the National Association of Black Journalists at Georgia State University.

Within Tyrik's career he has won many awards. He was awarded the 2018 Trailblazer award by the hit radio show, Let's Talk America. At Panther Report News he was awarded Best Hard News Reporter, Best Interview and Best All-Around News Reporter. He has also been presented awards for emceeing events.

Tyrik's end goal is to own a television and radio network so he can help young people get into the radio and TV industry.

Tyrik Wynn is available for bookings, to book him send an email to TyrikWynnBookings@gmail.com or simply call 754-225-2805

Tyrik Wynn's Social Media

Facebook: facebook.com/TyrikWynnTV

Instagram: @TyrikWynn_TV

Twitter: @TyrikWynnTV

www.ingramcontent.com/pod-product-compliance
Lightning Source LLC
Chambersburg PA
CBHW071124240526
45465CB00023B/812